BUILDING MOMENTUM

BUILDING MOMENTUM

A Decade of Construction, Renovation, and Renewal across the University of Illinois System

University of Illinois System
Foreword by TIMOTHY L. KILLEEN

UNIVERSITY OF ILLINOIS PRESS
Urbana, Chicago, and Springfield
www.press.uillinois.edu

Library of Congress Cataloging-in-Publication Data

Names: University of Illinois (System), author. | Killeen, T. L., author of foreword.

Title: Building momentum : a decade of construction, renovation, and renewal across the University of Illinois System / University of Illinois System ; foreword by Timothy L. Killeen.

Description: Urbana : University of Illinois Press, 2023. | Includes index.

Identifiers: LCCN 2023013046 (print) | LCCN 2023013047 (ebook) | ISBN 9780252045431 (cloth) | ISBN 9780252055034 (ebook)

Subjects: LCSH: University of Illinois (Urbana-Champaign campus)—Buildings. | University of Illinois Chicago Professional Colleges—Buildings. | University of Illinois Springfield—Buildings.

Classification: LCC LD2380 .U65 2023 (print) | LCC LD2380 (ebook) | DDC 378.773—dc23/eng/20230407

LC record available at https://lccn.loc.gov/2023013046

LC ebook record available at https://lccn.loc.gov/2023013047

CONTENTS

Part III. Healthcare

Part IV. Supporting Innovation

Part V. Athletics

Part VI. Upcoming Projects

FOREWORD

The University of Illinois System never stands still.

What began as a single, land-grant campus has grown to three best-in-class universities. Enrollment has surged from a handful of students when our doors first opened to more than 94,000 today. Academic and research programs have steadily evolved to meet ever-changing student needs and help lead our state and nation through fast-changing times.

And, thanks to an ambitious capital initiative launched in the summer of 2018, we have also ramped up efforts to ensure that our facilities keep pace with our excellence in education, discovery, and innovation.

We are well on our way toward the initiative's target of completing more than 500 capital projects valued at $4 billion over ten years. They include new, state-of-the-art buildings and major renovations that keep our facilities leading edge while preserving our history. And they are rising through a bigger toolbox of funding options, including public-private partnerships, thoughtful use of our capital reserves and bonding authority, and generous state capital funding after a decade of minimal or no state dollars for bricks-and-mortar work.

I hope you enjoy this look at the expanding footprint of Illinois' flagship university system—additions rooted in our commitment to driving progress and prosperity for the people of Illinois.

Timothy L. Killeen
President

ACKNOWLEDGMENTS

Thousands of talented and hardworking individuals contributed to the planning, design, construction, and completion of the projects represented in this volume, and the University of Illinois System extends thanks to all involved.

Special thanks to those who contributed to the creation of this book:

Special thanks to freelance writer Deb Aronson for her work on creating the text

Karen Greenwalt, University of Illinois System Office of the Vice President and Chief Financial Officer

Angela Jacobs, Michael A. Wilson, II, Ebone White, Sandra Yoo, University of Illinois System Office of Capital Programs

David Mercer, Kirsten Ruby, Gretchen Yordy, University of Illinois System External Relations and Communications

University of Illinois Press, University of Illinois System

University of Illinois Urbana-Champaign Division of Intercollegiate Athletics

University of Illinois Urbana-Champaign Strategic Communications and Marketing

University of Illinois Urbana-Champaign Facilities & Services, Capital Programs Division

University of Illinois Chicago, Planning, Sustainability and Project Management

University of Illinois Chicago Strategic Marketing and Communications

University of Illinois Springfield Facilities & Services, Campus Construction Unit

University of Illinois Springfield Marketing & Public Relations

Paul Ellinger, Vice President, CFO, and Comptroller, University of Illinois System

Avijit Ghosh, Executive Vice President and Vice President for Academic Affairs, University of Illinois System

Timothy L. Killeen, President, University of Illinois System

Special thanks to the talented photographers across the University of Illinois System: Hoss Fatemi, Michelle Hassell, Bob Ready, Clay Stalter, L. Brian Stauffer, Fred Zwicky

BUILDING MOMENTUM

PART I
Teaching and Research

ALTGELD HALL AND ILLINI HALL

Shining Brighter for the Future

College/Department: College of Liberal Arts & Sciences, Illinois Innovation Network

Architect: CannonDesign

Project Square Footage:
Altgeld—82,500 GSF; Illini Hall—128,314 GSF

Seeking LEED Platinum

Project Budget: $192,000,000

The renovation of Altgeld Hall and the replacement of Illini Hall with a new facility enables the University of Illinois Urbana-Champaign to honor its past and stride boldly into the future.

Altgeld Hall, the second-oldest building on the Main Quad, was built in response to a growth in campus population in the 1890s. Originally constructed as the Library Building, it also functioned as the Law Building before housing the Department of Mathematics since 1956. Meanwhile, Urbana is experiencing yet another period of exciting growth. Enrollment in the mathematics and statistics departments has more than doubled in the last decade. In addition, many programs outside the College of LAS require courses in math and statistics, further increasing enrollment in those courses by 40 percent over the same period.

Students from virtually every college on campus have taken a class or classes in Altgeld to lay a foundation for their careers. And if they've missed that experience, the melody of Altgeld's chimes ringing across campus brings beauty and joy to everyone's day. To maintain Altgeld Hall's importance on campus, it will be modernized, while its historic, architectural glories will be carefully and lovingly restored.

The 114-year-old Illini Hall, home of the Department of Statistics since 1985, will be replaced by a brand new six-story world-class facility for learning, innovation, and discovery in the mathematical sciences. The new space will feature a data science component—the future of data analysis—that does not currently exist on campus.

The Altgeld Hall and Illini Hall project was made possible in part through state funding of the Illinois Innovation Network, a state-wide network of research and innovation hubs that will serve as a magnet for technology and talent. Altgeld Hall and Illini Hall are part of the Urbana-Champaign–based IIN hub.

Ultimately, these new and renovated facilities enable the outstanding programs housed in them to shine brighter, energizing and inspiring current and prospective students and faculty and making the entire campus proud.

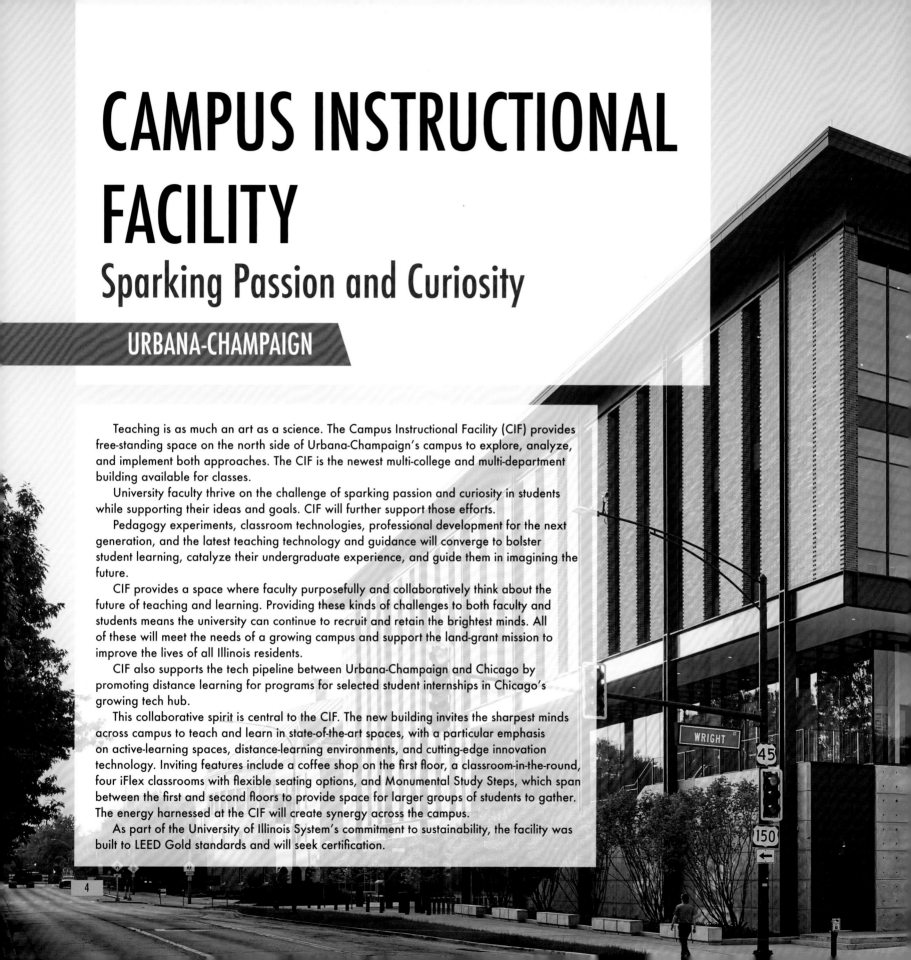

CAMPUS INSTRUCTIONAL FACILITY
Sparking Passion and Curiosity

URBANA-CHAMPAIGN

Teaching is as much an art as a science. The Campus Instructional Facility (CIF) provides free-standing space on the north side of Urbana-Champaign's campus to explore, analyze, and implement both approaches. The CIF is the newest multi-college and multi-department building available for classes.

University faculty thrive on the challenge of sparking passion and curiosity in students while supporting their ideas and goals. CIF will further support those efforts.

Pedagogy experiments, classroom technologies, professional development for the next generation, and the latest teaching technology and guidance will converge to bolster student learning, catalyze their undergraduate experience, and guide them in imagining the future.

CIF provides a space where faculty purposefully and collaboratively think about the future of teaching and learning. Providing these kinds of challenges to both faculty and students means the university can continue to recruit and retain the brightest minds. All of these will meet the needs of a growing campus and support the land-grant mission to improve the lives of all Illinois residents.

CIF also supports the tech pipeline between Urbana-Champaign and Chicago by promoting distance learning for programs for selected student internships in Chicago's growing tech hub.

This collaborative spirit is central to the CIF. The new building invites the sharpest minds across campus to teach and learn in state-of-the-art spaces, with a particular emphasis on active-learning spaces, distance-learning environments, and cutting-edge innovation technology. Inviting features include a coffee shop on the first floor, a classroom-in-the-round, four iFlex classrooms with flexible seating options, and Monumental Study Steps, which span between the first and second floors to provide space for larger groups of students to gather. The energy harnessed at the CIF will create synergy across the campus.

As part of the University of Illinois System's commitment to sustainability, the facility was built to LEED Gold standards and will seek certification.

College/Department: Multi-disciplinary
Architect: Skidmore, Owings & Merrill
Project Square Footage: 124,000 GSF
Seeking LEED Platinum and Net Zero energy
Project Budget: $75,000,000

SIDNEY LU MECHANICAL ENGINEERING BUILDING

Overhauled and Invigorated

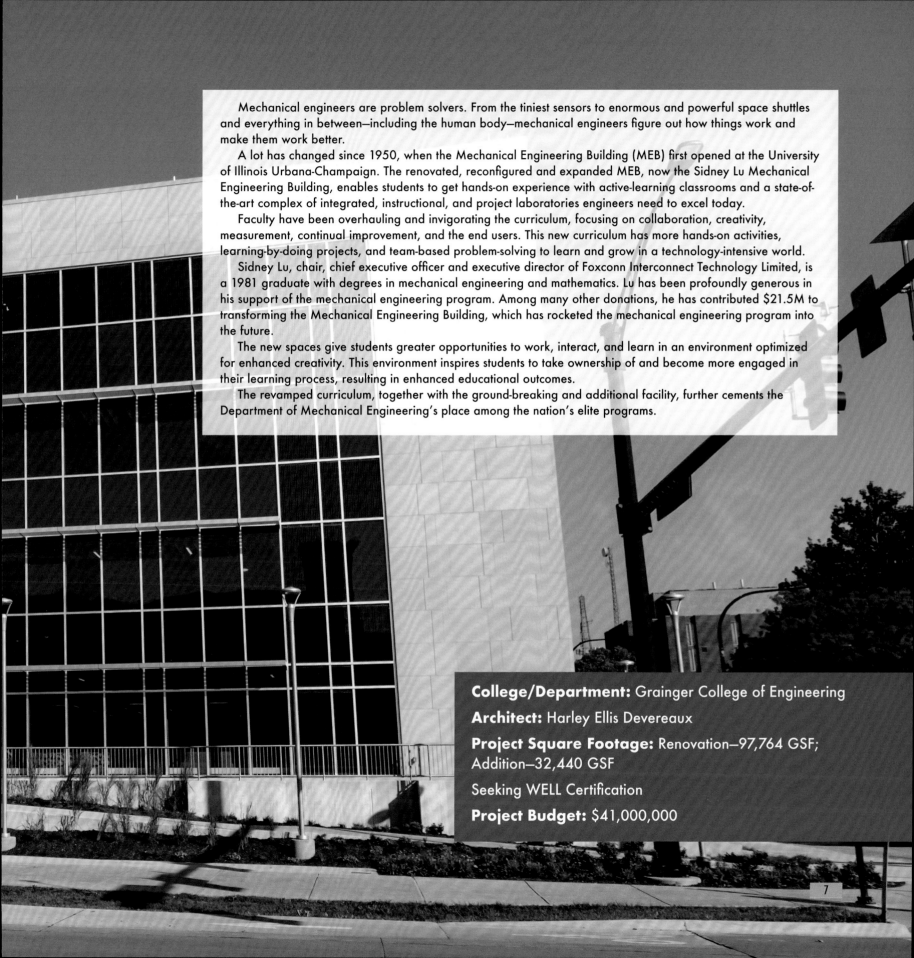

Mechanical engineers are problem solvers. From the tiniest sensors to enormous and powerful space shuttles and everything in between—including the human body—mechanical engineers figure out how things work and make them work better.

A lot has changed since 1950, when the Mechanical Engineering Building (MEB) first opened at the University of Illinois Urbana-Champaign. The renovated, reconfigured and expanded MEB, now the Sidney Lu Mechanical Engineering Building, enables students to get hands-on experience with active-learning classrooms and a state-of-the-art complex of integrated, instructional, and project laboratories engineers need to excel today.

Faculty have been overhauling and invigorating the curriculum, focusing on collaboration, creativity, measurement, continual improvement, and the end users. This new curriculum has more hands-on activities, learning-by-doing projects, and team-based problem-solving to learn and grow in a technology-intensive world.

Sidney Lu, chair, chief executive officer and executive director of Foxconn Interconnect Technology Limited, is a 1981 graduate with degrees in mechanical engineering and mathematics. Lu has been profoundly generous in his support of the mechanical engineering program. Among many other donations, he has contributed $21.5M to transforming the Mechanical Engineering Building, which has rocketed the mechanical engineering program into the future.

The new spaces give students greater opportunities to work, interact, and learn in an environment optimized for enhanced creativity. This environment inspires students to take ownership of and become more engaged in their learning process, resulting in enhanced educational outcomes.

The revamped curriculum, together with the ground-breaking and additional facility, further cements the Department of Mechanical Engineering's place among the nation's elite programs.

College/Department: Grainger College of Engineering

Architect: Harley Ellis Devereaux

Project Square Footage: Renovation—97,764 GSF; Addition—32,440 GSF

Seeking WELL Certification

Project Budget: $41,000,000

RICHARD D. AND ANNE MARIE IRWIN DOCTORAL STUDY HALL

A Rare Gem

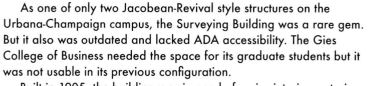

College/Department: Gies College of Business

Architect: Shive-Hattery

Project Square Footage: 8,232 GSF

Certified LEED Gold

Project Budget: $7,750,000

As one of only two Jacobean-Revival style structures on the Urbana-Champaign campus, the Surveying Building was a rare gem. But it also was outdated and lacked ADA accessibility. The Gies College of Business needed the space for its graduate students but it was not usable in its previous configuration.

Built in 1905, the building was in need of major interior, exterior, and structural improvements.

It was important to both retain the building's historic charm and create an up-to-date space for business doctoral and postdoctoral scholars to pursue their research and teaching activities.

Insulation was applied to the underside of the roof to improve the building envelope's energy efficiency and thermal properties. Historic window and door replacement, a complete slate roof replacement, repair of exterior wood details, masonry repair and tuckpointing, and a redesigned entrance with a new ADA-compliant ramp completed the exterior renovation.

The interior now accommodates up to 100 doctoral students. Work spaces and social gathering areas have been designed for the accountancy, business administration, and finance departments. A conference room, two kitchenettes, and two advising offices also were created from the original interior. The two small basements were excavated to create one large space complete with egress stair towers and an elevator to comply with ADA standards.

Now known as the University of Illinois Urbana-Champaign Richard D. and Anne Marie Irwin Doctoral Study Hall, the building now has the best of both worlds: a historic exterior with unique details and an interior that offers modern workspaces and ADA-compliant accessibility.

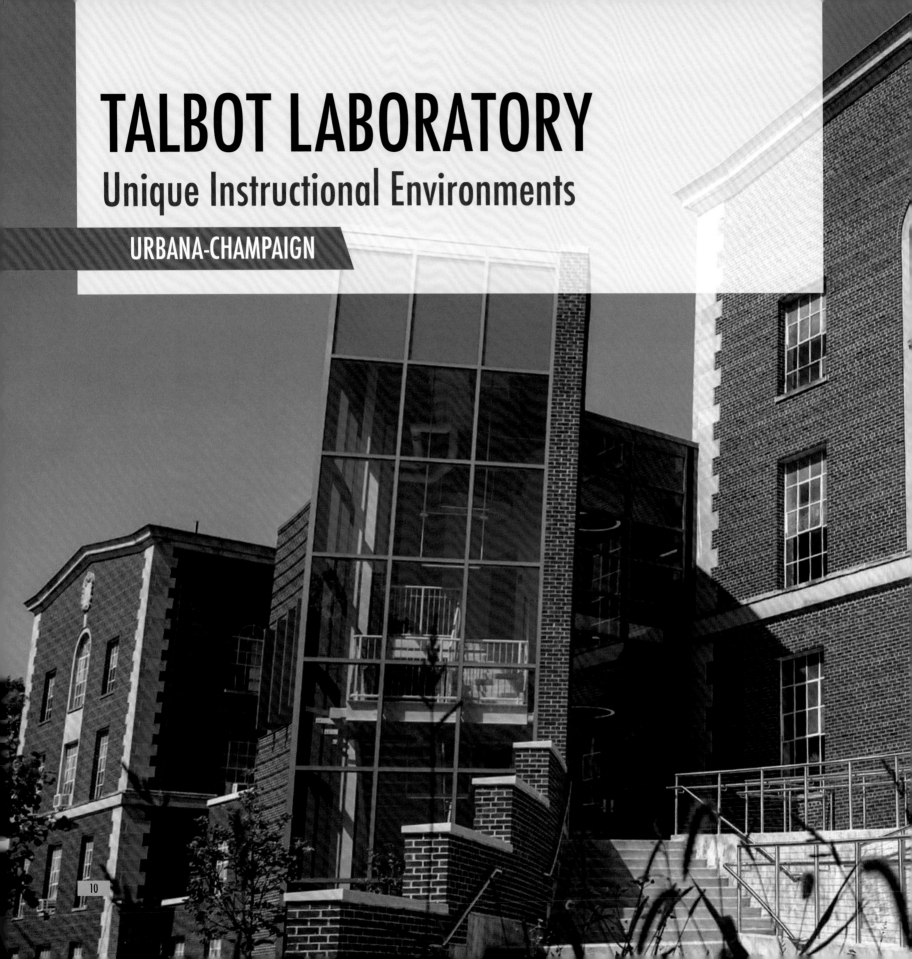

TALBOT LABORATORY
Unique Instructional Environments
URBANA-CHAMPAIGN

College/Department: Grainger College of Engineering

Architect: EXP

Project Square Footage: Renovation—9,200 GSF; Addition—9,404 GSF

Seeking LEED Gold

Project Budget: $8,660,000

The approximately 9,404-square-foot addition to Talbot Laboratory (one of the oldest buildings within the University of Illinois Urbana-Champaign's Grainger College of Engineering) is part of an ongoing effort to increase and improve students' hands-on experiences in the departments of Aerospace Engineering (AE) and Nuclear, Plasma and Radiological Engineering (NPRE).

The upgrade creates a unique instructional environment where concepts can be experienced in virtual and real spaces. These opportunities enable a more comprehensive understanding of the underlying principles introduced in lectures.

With an instructional composites manufacturing laboratory and space to learn additive manufacturing and 3D printing, AE students will hit the ground running and start their careers innovating. The renovation and addition also includes space to learn nano-satellite design, assembling, testing, and operation.

Students in the NPRE department will benefit from an instructional radiation measurements laboratory and a nuclear materials laboratory. These facilities will also support the growing number of students in nuclear medical imaging and therapeutic technologies, two fields that provide outstanding employment opportunities.

The Talbot upgrades provide unique facilities not previously available at the Grainger College of Engineering. They will substantially improve the experience of undergraduate and graduate students not only in AE and NPRE but throughout the Grainger College of Engineering. The project further consolidates Urbana-Champaign's position as a hands-on engineering education leader.

The new facilities and equipment will ensure that graduates have the best training and education as they enter the workforce or continue on for an advanced degree.

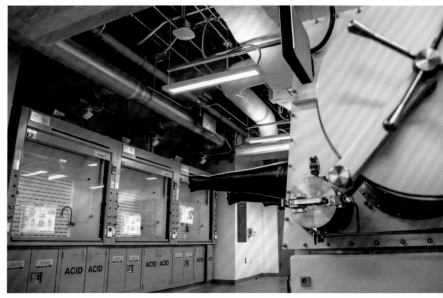

CIVIL AND ENVIRONMENTAL ENGINEERING BUILDING— HYDROSYSTEMS LABORATORY

Supporting Innovative Teaching and Learning

URBANA-CHAMPAIGN

College/Department: Grainger College of Engineering

Architect: Reifsteck Reid & Company Architects

Project Square Footage: Renovation–4,000 GSF; Addition–45,000 GSF

Seeking LEED Gold

Project Budget: $35,600,000

The expansion and renovation of Urbana-Champaign's Civil and Environmental Engineering (CEE) Department's Hydrosystems Laboratory modernizes instructional facilities and makes research into cutting-edge sustainable solutions possible. Modern classrooms, laboratories, and collaboration areas were designed to support innovative teaching methods like project-based learning, hands-on experimentation, and group work.

The Hydrosystems Laboratory has been expanded from one level to a basement topped by three floors and a mechanical penthouse. In addition, a smart bridge extends from the third floor of the addition to Newmark Laboratory.

This enclosed pedestrian suspension bridge will function as a living laboratory to teach students about the effects of dynamic forces on the built environment. A dense array of high-fidelity accelerometer sensors will provide a full set of data from which accurate vibration motions can be computed and linked to weather, pedestrian traffic, or other structural stimuli. Vibration records can be used to estimate the structural properties and improve analysis models of the bridge. Additionally, two displacement sensors will be installed—one each on the north and south expansion joints of the bridge—to monitor the movement of the bridge.

Sensors to measure and monitor temperature and strains within the foundations will help researchers and students monitor and understand how the geothermal heating and cooling system is performing. The new facility provides opportunities for both research and instruction in sustainable solutions.

Consistent with the University of Illinois System's commitment to sustainability, the Hydrosystems Laboratory is built to LEED Silver standards.

It is a rare building that provides not only state-of-the-art facilities but also a hands-on, real-time laboratory for budding engineers, all in an environmentally responsible way. The Hydrosystems Laboratory does just that, making students graduating from the program highly prepared to be part of the global solution.

NATURAL HISTORY BUILDING
A Beloved Landmark

URBANA-CHAMPAIGN

College/Department: College of Liberal Arts & Sciences

Architect: LCM Architects

Project Square Footage: 156,000 GSF

Certified LEED Gold

Project Budget: $78,426,395

With a massive renovation, this historic and beloved landmark building has been repurposed into a twenty-first-century learning and teaching facility. The Natural History Building (NHB), which was built in 1892, is the third-oldest building on Urbana-Champaign's campus. Its architectural details earned it a place on the National Register of Historic Places.

In 2017, the NHB reopened and now provides an inspirational, welcoming, and modern facility, with vibrant community hubs, including a breathtaking vaulted chamber on the third floor. In addition, the facility is now fully accessible.

Completing this project has enabled all programs within the School of Earth, Society and Environment to be housed under one roof for the first time, joining the School of Integrative Biology in the building.

The NHB hosts classes for more than 20,000 students per year, and the building now features a plethora of modern and flexible classroom spaces, as well as provides innovative and transformational learning experiences through:

- state-of-the-art laboratories for advanced courses and specialized research in areas including geophysics, geochemistry, sedimentology, earth materials, geomicrobiology, and remote sensing,

- computer labs where students work with the latest geographic and remote-sensing data, model the Earth System, and explore mathematical models of biological processes,

- a visualization studio where researchers can perform tasks such as analyzing satellite weather data to look into the eye of a hurricane or analyzing satellite space mission data with NASA,

- and specialized teaching facilities where students can learn how to build analytical instruments that can be used for microscopic analysis of earth materials, visualizing big data using geographic information systems, and other projects.

As part of the University of Illinois System's commitment to sustainability, the NHB has earned a Gold LEED certification.

ENGINEERING INNOVATION BUILDING

Attracting Top Academic Talent

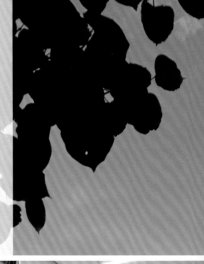

Enrollment at the UIC College of Engineering has almost doubled in the last 10 years and grown to more than 5,000 students in the last few years. The Engineering Innovation Building supports this enormous growth while providing unique learning opportunities for students, attracting top academic talent and strengthening ties with local businesses and industry in the Chicagoland area.

The new building includes research, classroom and office space, and brings the chemical engineering department, which has been off campus for over 20 years, into the center of the east campus.

Our nation's bridges, roads, and water pipes are aging, and engineers have an extraordinary opportunity to improve our infrastructure. The Engineering Innovation Building's high-bay structural research lab is a unique facility in northern Illinois. Here, researchers and government agencies can develop and test large-scale structural components and determine how they behave under various loads and conditions. The state-of-the-art laboratory will attract renowned researchers, energetic students, and forward-thinking companies to develop damage-detection sensors that generate big data on structural degradation and develop revolutionary new materials that will allow new structural designs for buildings and bridges.

In addition to addressing infrastructure needs, students in the Engineering Innovation Building can learn to address water and energy needs via membrane purification, artificial photosynthesis, molecular photovoltaics, thermal batteries and fuel cells, as well as drug delivery, cancer detection biocompatible surfaces, complex fluids, 3D printing, and nanoelectronics.

These opportunities and experiences will enable UIC engineering students to improve the world around them while enjoying a challenging and rewarding career.

College/Department: College of Engineering
Architect: Dewberry
Project Square Footage: 57,433 GSF
Certified LEED Gold
Project Budget: $43,000,000

EVERITT LABORATORY
Improving the Human Condition

URBANA-CHAMPAIGN

College/Department: Grainger College of Engineering

Architect: BSA Lifestructures

Project Square Footage: 124,256 GSF

Certified LEED Gold

Project Budget: $51,195,875

Following a two-year, multimillion-dollar renovation, Everitt Laboratory—former home of the Department of Electrical and Computer Engineering—reopened in June 2018 as the new home of Urbana-Champaign's Bioengineering Department, which has grown significantly over the last decade. The 125,000 square feet of renovated space includes research and instructional labs, classrooms, computer labs, and collaboration spaces for more than 220 faculty, graduate students, post-docs, and staff members—all housed in one building for the first time.

The bioengineering curriculum combines biology and engineering principles to help students understand how human biological systems function. Students also use an interdisciplinary and technology-based approach to identify, define, and solve problems, including grand challenges in health and medicine.

Built to LEED Gold standards, Everitt Laboratory provides students and faculty with state-of-the-art instructional and research facilities, where they can learn, create, and innovate, all to improve the human condition.

Speaking of grand challenges in health and medicine, the Department of Bioengineering works closely with the new Carle Illinois College of Medicine, the campus's engineering-based medical college. Everitt is home to the Jump Simulation Center, where medical students use the latest medical equipment and simulation technology to train in an array of areas, including surgery, intensive care, and clinical skills. Bioengineering students also use the Sim Center for design, capstone, professional master's, and research projects.

The Everitt Laboratory renovation is a significant step forward in the University of Illinois System's effort to continue attracting and retaining outstanding researchers, faculty, and students to address grand challenges of our age.

ELECTRICAL AND COMPUTER ENGINEERING BUILDING
Designed to Inspire

College/Department: Grainger College of Engineering

Architect: SmithGroup

Project Square Footage: 162,000 GSF

Certified LEED Gold

Project Budget: $96,734,000

The new building for the Department of Electrical and Computer Engineering at the University of Illinois Urbana-Champaign (ECE Illinois) opened in 2014 and is the epicenter of new technology and groundbreaking innovation.

The expansive, five-story building consolidates the university's nationally ranked department, which had been housed for more than 60 years at the circa-1948 Everitt Laboratory. The new building provides 45 instructional and research labs, 48 private faculty offices, and 280 graduate student workstations. Among its most noteworthy spaces are a 4,000-square-foot instructional clean room and a 400-seat auditorium, now one of the largest gathering spaces on campus.

Keeping with ECE Illinois's dedication to pushing the limits of technical innovation, energy efficiency was not only a priority but a driver for the project. With the goal of Net Zero Energy—meaning the building aims to produce as much energy as it uses—the facility has been built to the highest LEED designation: platinum.

Intended to go beyond a collection of bricks and mortar, the ECE building is a place where curiosity is celebrated and intellectual collisions occur naturally. Designed to inspire and support interdisciplinary learning and research and driven by societal needs and opportunities, this high-performance facility is the direct result of integrating culture, energy research, and architecture.

With these new facilities, ECE Illinois will continue to educate leaders in the field for generations to come.

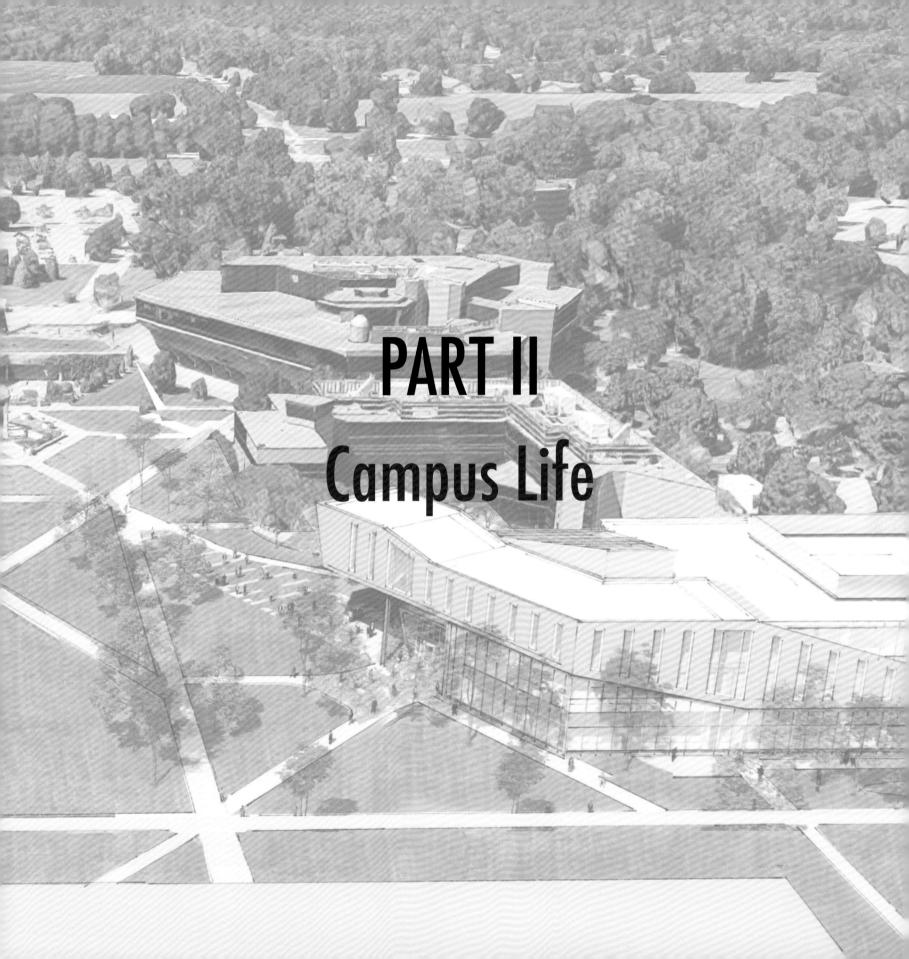

PART II
Campus Life

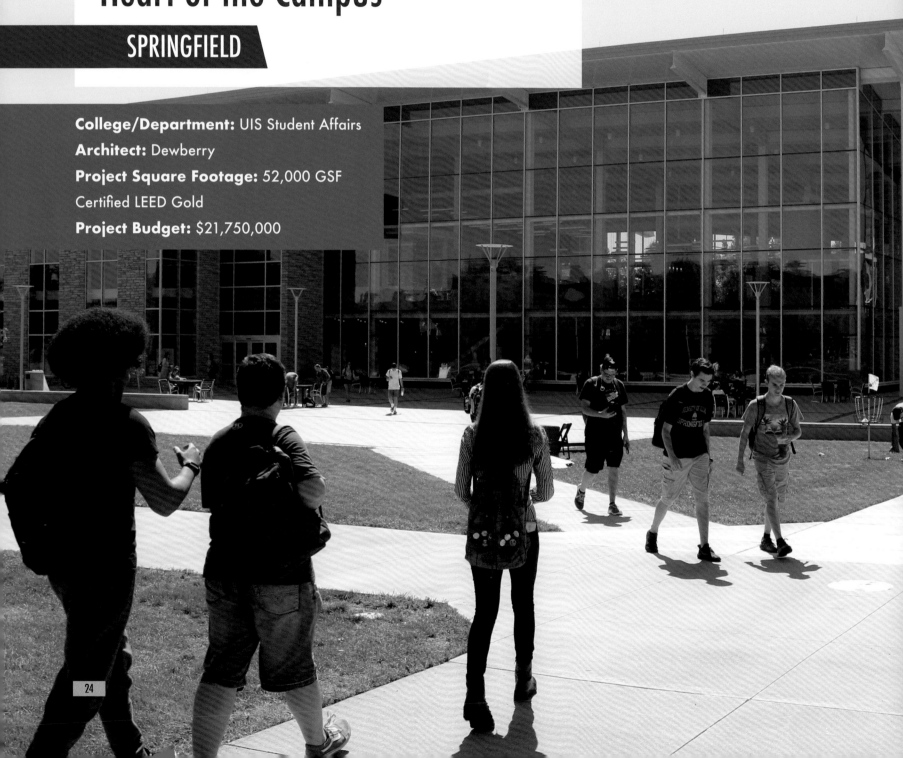

STUDENT UNION
Heart of the Campus

College/Department: UIS Student Affairs
Architect: Dewberry
Project Square Footage: 52,000 GSF
Certified LEED Gold
Project Budget: $21,750,000

Since the two-story, 52,000-square-foot University of Illinois Springfield Student Union opened in 2018 it has become the heart of the campus. As a place to gather formally and informally, the student union fills a need that has been growing since the campus joined the UI system in 1995.

Located at the crossroads of campus, the building has become a destination for virtually everyone who comes to UIS, a place "to see and be seen." The facility houses lounges, dining options, large multipurpose spaces, and the Student Leadership Center, which includes student government, volunteer offices, and workspaces for student organizations.

The building's open design enhances its social nature. With its expansive windows, outside terraces, and overlapping functions inside, visitors to the student union are afforded views to, from, and all around the building. A two-story open lounge connects the building's interior spaces, thus creating a dynamic heart for the building and campus.

As part of the University of Illinois System's commitment to sustainability, the student union has been built to LEED Gold standards, and includes a green roof with almost 200,000 plants over a sloped membrane and a rainwater reclamation system to reduce storm runoff and limit the need for irrigation.

ACADEMIC AND RESIDENTIAL COMPLEX
Revitalizing Campus Housing

CHICAGO

College/Department: Campus Housing

Architect: Solomon Cordwell Buenz

Project Square Footage: 200,000 GSF

Certified LEED Gold

Project Budget: $100,000,000

At Chicago's largest university and only public research university, the latest residential hall revitalizes campus housing and provides much-needed amenities to UIC students.

College isn't only about learning course content; it's about interacting with fellow students, living independently for the first time, and making connections that will last a lifetime. UIC's Academic and Residential Complex (ARC) sets the stage for success by providing a beautiful new facility that sends the message, "You are important. You deserve the best. We are here for you."

The new facility includes a 10-story, 200,000-square-foot residential component with housing space for approximately 550 students, as well as a fitness center, multiple social and gaming lounges, study lounges, and laundry facilities.

The most dramatic feature is a breathtaking tenth-floor sky lounge with an impressive view of downtown Chicago. This view reminds students they are part of a larger world and their academic success will launch them into that world.

The two-story, 52,000-square-foot academic classroom portion of the building has space for lectures, active learning, small group learning, and more. Break-out areas throughout the building encourage collaboration among students and help foster faculty-student interactions.

Designed with a "nod to Netsch," the original architect of the campus, the building's façade and interiors echo the geometric movement expressed in Walter Netsch's distinctive architecture. Always mindful of sustainability goals, the LEED Gold-certified building is sited for optimal solar orientation to mitigate heat gain.

This project is financed entirely by a private partner, American Campus Communities, in the first "public-private partnership" (P3) of its kind in Illinois.

LIBRARY COMMONS
Energizing Addition to Campus

College/Department: Multi-disciplinary
Architect: Bailey Edward Design
Project Square Footage: 63,500 GSF
Seeking LEED Gold
Project Budget: $35,000,000

Located on the main quad, the Library Commons' central location will complete the University of Illinois Springfield campus's academic core. The brick in its façade is designed to mirror its neighboring academic buildings, while glass and metal panels will create extra visual interest. Large windows will let in plenty of daylight, promoting improved mental well-being for all who enter the building. The facility's design will make it an attractive, welcoming, and energizing addition to the campus, engaging with students and faculty alike to promote interactions, learning, and community. The Library Commons—the library, re-imagined—is a space in which reflective thinking and quiet study will co-exist with collaborative spaces and group study areas. At the heart of the Library Commons, an open "useful stair" will spiral its way up the building's three floors, each landing opening up into informal and fully accessible gathering areas. The end of the spiral makes its way to the main library's Collection and Reading Room, including a study space with panoramic views of the campus's main quad, allowing students to focus and reflect. The Library Commons' spaces

and resources will inspire new and innovative teaching techniques, support the skill sets required for higher learning, encourage collaboration in research and instruction, and accommodate a variety of uses and purposes. In addition, the building will house Information Technology Services (ITS), the Career Development Center, the Center for Academic Success and Advising (CASA), and several experiential teaching-learning labs and high-tech classrooms. Given the critical role the library, CASA, ITS, and the Career Development Center play in student learning, the synergy created by co-locating these units is a force multiplier in academic success. In the future, the Library Commons will serve as a vital part of UIS' academic mission to engage, support, and collaborate with students in every stage of their journey. Because of the University of Illinois System's commitment to sustainability, the facility has been designed to achieve the US Green Building Council's Gold standard for Leadership in Energy and Environmental Design (LEED), and, as such, will be a beloved and much-used resource on this vibrant campus for decades to come.

CHEZ VETERANS CENTER
Support and Commitment to Veterans

College/Department: College of Applied Health Sciences

Architect: LCM Architects

Project Square Footage: 31,670 GSF

Certified LEED Gold

Project Budget: $14,000,000

Transitioning to college can be challenging for anyone, but for those who are arriving after having served in the military, the experience—shifting from an externally structured life to one in which structure is all self-imposed—can be even harder.

Chez Veterans Center (CVC), which opened in 2015, provides a setting to help with that transition for student veterans and their families, particularly those veterans with service-related impairments and long-term disabilities. In this regard, CVC is part of Urbana-Champaign's long history of leadership and passionate commitment to students with disabilities.

The Chez Veterans Center provides an array of resources, including, but not limited to, academic coaching; individual, group, couples and family counseling; and neuropsychological testing.

The building is open and inviting and includes classrooms and computer labs, research space, a well-equipped gym, fully functional kitchen, study rooms, lounges, residential rooms, staff offices, and even playrooms for children.

The CVC is the only student veterans' center in the country to house residential and service functions in one structure. Residential units have been designed and equipped to accommodate student veterans with severe disabilities, creating a supportive and customized setting for academic success.

The CVC enables veterans to have a meaningful college experience, and their presence on campus diversifies the student population, creating a more profound and inclusive experience for everyone.

BRUCE D. NESBITT AFRICAN AMERICAN CULTURAL CENTER
Inclusive Sanctuary of Learning and Support

College/Department: Student Affairs, Office of Inclusion and Intercultural Relations

Architect: Interactive Design Architects

Project Square Footage: 8,200 GSF

Seeking LEED Silver

Project Budget: $5,900,000

The new Bruce D. Nesbitt African American Cultural Center (BNAACC), a vibrant and distinctive building, provides a sanctuary of learning and support, helps create a culturally respectful campus environment, promotes African American culture through performing arts, and provides leadership and professional opportunities for students.

First created in 1969, the Afro-American Cultural Program had a few temporary homes over the years. With the opening of the BNAACC in 2019, the program has a dedicated building. The building honors Bruce Nesbitt, a beloved and respected leader and counselor, who served as program director from 1974–1996.

The center and its programs serve more than 3,000 undergraduate and graduate students, including many students who identify as multiracial and international. The program also conducts outreach to the local community and plays an active role in recruiting new students.

The BNAACC provides African American students with an inclusive space where their cultures, identities, and norms are understood and where students' backgrounds, values, beliefs, and experiences are celebrated.

The building's location close to the Urbana-Champaign Main Quad makes it easy for students to stop by between classes. Students can gather in the atrium and multipurpose room on the main floor or use a yoga/dance studio or the media center in the basement. The building also has smaller rooms for quiet study and a full kitchen.

The building's multihued bricks make a bold design statement, symbolizing the diversity of the university community, joined together in a display of inclusiveness.

The building design team, Interactive Design Architects, was led by Urbana alumna Dina Griffin.

ILLINOIS STREET RESIDENCE HALLS: TOWNSEND AND WARDALL

Massive Upgrades (Many Hidden) Make All the Difference

URBANA-CHAMPAIGN

College/Department: University Housing
Architect: CannonDesign
Project Square Footage: 220,676 GSF
LEED Silver
Project Budget: $67,500,000

It's as if Townsend and Wardall halls, long beloved and like the Velveteen Rabbit, a bit love worn, were sent to the spa and returned a better, brighter, and happier version of themselves.

These two residence halls, Townsend and Wardall, adjoining the Illinois Street Residence Halls (ISR) Dining Hall, were built in 1962 and have not been significantly upgraded until now. The University of Illinois Urbana-Champaign undertook an effort to completely modernize the facility in visible and environmental ways.

The construction project completely upgraded the entire mechanical temperature control and ventilation system, adding air conditioning and allowing for individual room temperature control. The original windows and associated panels were replaced with a new highly insulated system. The original bathrooms and shower rooms were remodeled into individual private bathrooms for greater student privacy. New doors, lighting, paint, and carpet help the spaces feel much more comfortable.

This project has had an enormous impact, considering that the two residence halls house 1,100 students.

After 60 years and more than 60,000 students calling these buildings their home, Townsend and Wardall provide an outstanding first impression on both prospective and incoming students and their families. The more comfortable environment and updated amenities make visitors and residents alike linger and enjoy their surroundings.

35

ILLINOIS STREET RESIDENCE HALLS DINING FACILITY

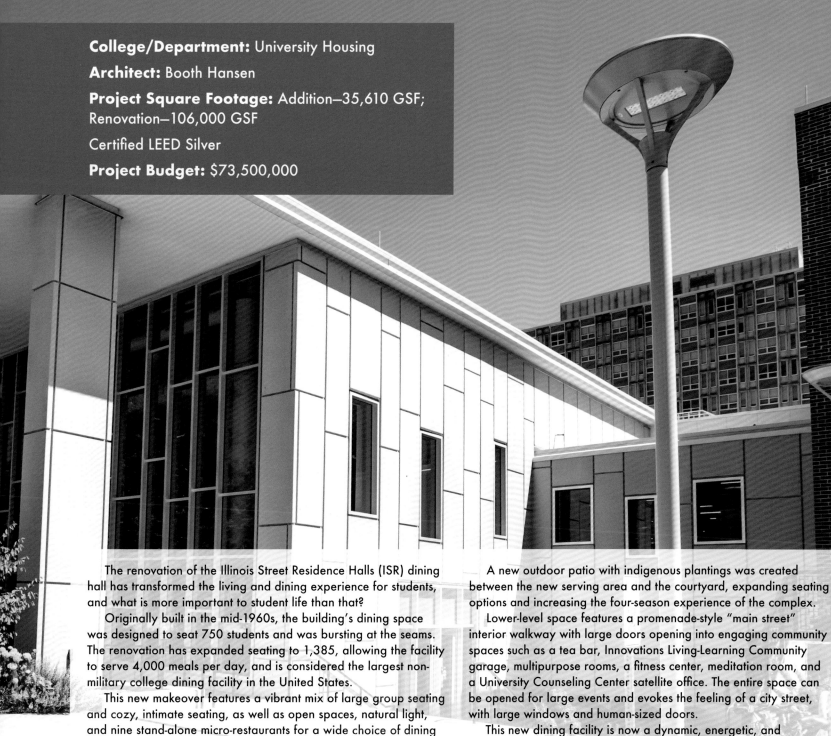

College/Department: University Housing

Architect: Booth Hansen

Project Square Footage: Addition—35,610 GSF; Renovation—106,000 GSF

Certified LEED Silver

Project Budget: $73,500,000

The renovation of the Illinois Street Residence Halls (ISR) dining hall has transformed the living and dining experience for students, and what is more important to student life than that?

Originally built in the mid-1960s, the building's dining space was designed to seat 750 students and was bursting at the seams. The renovation has expanded seating to 1,385, allowing the facility to serve 4,000 meals per day, and is considered the largest non-military college dining facility in the United States.

This new makeover features a vibrant mix of large group seating and cozy, intimate seating, as well as open spaces, natural light, and nine stand-alone micro-restaurants for a wide choice of dining options. Those options include vegetarian and allergen free as well as international foods reflective of the student population's diversity, plus comfort food like hamburgers and other American diner cuisine.

A new outdoor patio with indigenous plantings was created between the new serving area and the courtyard, expanding seating options and increasing the four-season experience of the complex.

Lower-level space features a promenade-style "main street" interior walkway with large doors opening into engaging community spaces such as a tea bar, Innovations Living-Learning Community garage, multipurpose rooms, a fitness center, meditation room, and a University Counseling Center satellite office. The entire space can be opened for large events and evokes the feeling of a city street, with large windows and human-sized doors.

This new dining facility is now a dynamic, energetic, and highly functional space that underscores and highlights feelings of community and camaraderie that University Housing strives to create for all residents.

Wassaja Hall, which opened in 2016, is the third new residence hall constructed in Urbana-Champaign's Ikenberry Commons neighborhood to replace outdated campus housing.

With 504 beds, multiple single-gender bathrooms per floor, individually controlled A/C and rooms clustered in "pods," Wassaja offers both a more private and community-oriented experience. The 152,753-square-foot building is completely accessible.

By making the hall available to returning as well as first-year students, everyone benefits from interacting with those outside their own year.

A residence hall by any other name is still a residence hall, but naming this hall for an alumnus whose accomplishments had been lost in the sands of time encourages the entire university community to learn about and honor Wassaja, the first Indigenous person and first person of color to graduate from the university. Wassaja, who graduated in 1884 (and was class president), was a member of the Yavapai-Apache Nation tribe. He was renamed Carlos Montezuma by his adoptive father. He went on to first earn a medical degree from Northwestern University and then become a tireless advocate for Indigenous people.

The choice of name is part of an ongoing effort by the university to recognize and celebrate diversity that is part of its history, though not always recognized. The trio of massive weathered steel, stylized baskets lining the path to the entrance explicitly celebrate and honor Wassaja's native roots and evoke the artistry of Yavapai basketry. The stone bases on which each basket is placed were sourced from Arizona near his birthplace.

As part of the University of Illinois System's commitment to sustainability, Wassaja Hall is LEED Gold certified. Committed to resident-centered design, the furniture and finishes were chosen based on student feedback.

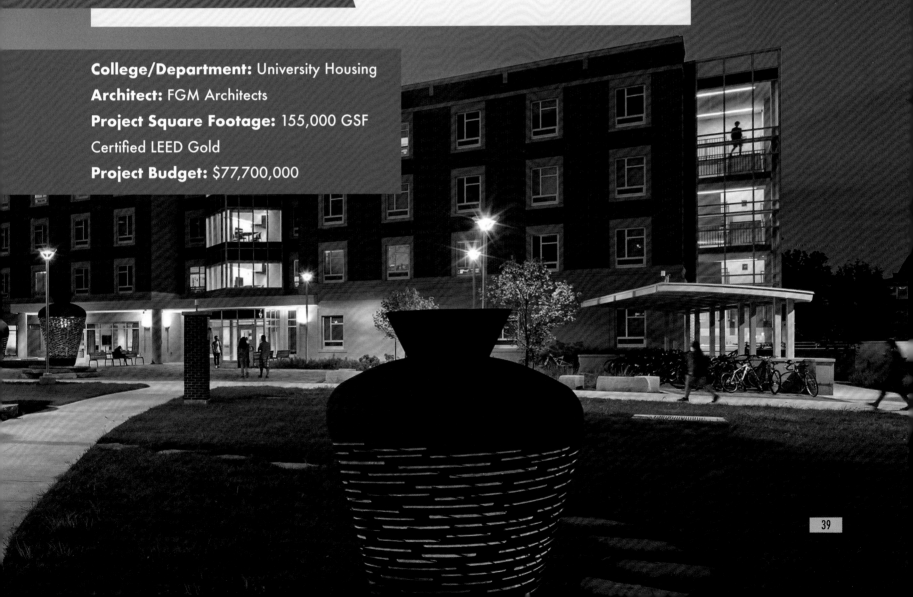

IKENBERRY COMMONS: WASSAJA HALL
Celebrating a Remarkable Alumnus

URBANA-CHAMPAIGN

College/Department: University Housing
Architect: FGM Architects
Project Square Footage: 155,000 GSF
Certified LEED Gold
Project Budget: $77,700,000

IKENBERRY COMMONS: BOUSFIELD HALL
Strength and Resilience

URBANA-CHAMPAIGN

College/Department: University Housing

Architect: FGM Architects

Project Square Footage: 58,500 GSF

Certified LEED Platinum

Project Budget: $63,944,555

Campus residence halls provide a home away from home for students, who are, after all, at the heart of the university's core mission. A hall must balance individual needs and provide opportunities to mingle and meet other students but not be so chaotic that there is no peace and privacy. While providing a quiet and stable environment, it should not be so quiet that students end up feeling isolated. It's a fine balance.

Bousfield Hall strikes that balance. This is the first residence hall on campus to have suite-style residence space. The building also features a multipurpose room, a rec room, and laundry. The new residence hall, built in 2013, is fully accessible and includes a dedicated suite for students with severe physical disabilities who require assistance in the activities of daily living.

Designed to meet LEED Platinum standards, Bousfield's design optimizes energy performance and provides a high level of individual environmental control, including meters on each floor so students can observe their energy usage.

But Bousfield Hall does much more: it recognizes Maudelle Tanner Brown Bousfield. Ms. Bousfield was the first African American woman to graduate from the University of Illinois Urbana-Champaign. From 1903 to 1905, she was the only Black woman on campus and graduated with honors in 1906.

Naming the hall in her honor educated everyone—students, staff, faculty, visitors, and the wider community—about what a Black woman achieved in an era when so many barriers existed.

Maudelle Bousfield's strength and resilience inspires many students who learn of her story, thanks to the naming of the facility in her honor.

PART III
Healthcare

UI HEALTH WELCOME ATRIUM
Improving Access and Comfort

CHICAGO

College/Department: UI Health

Architect: Moody Nolan

Project Square Footage: Renovation–8,000 GSF; Addition–12,000 GSF

Seeking LEED Silver

Project Budget: $18,000,000

The new 20,000-square-foot lobby at the University of Illinois Hospital is a dramatic, light-filled atrium that elevates the visibility of the hospital while creating a welcoming and calming atmosphere.

Because the University of Illinois Hospital & Health Sciences System (UI Health) partners with the Mile Square Health Center, a network of Federally Qualified Health Centers that focus on providing top-quality care in community-based healthcare centers, the atrium project has been especially important to make hospital visits less stressful for populations that have historically felt unheard, unwelcome, and underserved.

The lobby is a two-story addition that serves as the main entrance to the hospital. The first floor includes a custom-designed reception desk, security station, elevators to the second floor, a communicating stair, comfortable seating areas for visitors and patients, and planters filled with restful greenery.

The second floor includes a contemplation space for quiet reflection and prayer, the office for Pastoral Care Services, as well as conference rooms and additional seating. The UI Health Specialty Care Building also is accessible via a skywalk.

Hospital spaces can also feel confusing, and the renovation features improved access, circulation, and wayfinding for patients, their families, other visitors, and staff. The lobby's ambience is modern and welcoming for everyone who walks through the doors.

This lobby improves the patient experience and elevates the UI Health brand. Its open and inviting exterior makes the atrium part of the community in which it is located. The Welcome Atrium project is on track to receive a Gold LEED certificate.

The atrium provides a welcoming and less stressful hospital experience for patients and visitors, while reducing energy use.

45

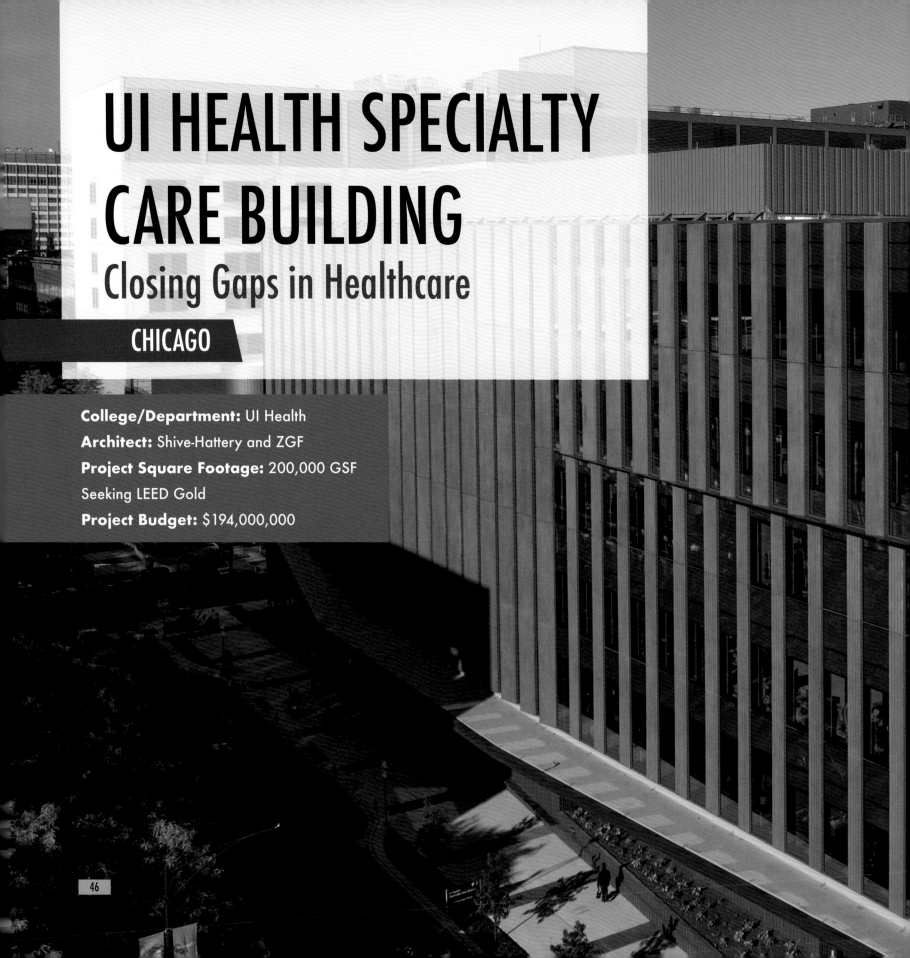

UI HEALTH SPECIALTY CARE BUILDING
Closing Gaps in Healthcare

College/Department: UI Health
Architect: Shive-Hattery and ZGF
Project Square Footage: 200,000 GSF
Seeking LEED Gold
Project Budget: $194,000,000

The new $194 million, 200,000-square-foot UI Health Specialty Care Building (SCB) is the first new building for the University of Illinois Chicago's academic and clinical health enterprise, UI Health, since 2014.

The facility provides a more efficient, comfortable, and patient-friendly home for specialty care. The new building is spacious and state-of-the-art, enabling many of UI Health's clinical programs to handle increased demand for care, including for outpatient surgery.

In addition, the Specialty Care Building will help provide a platform to address the inequities of access on the west and south sides of Chicago. That inequity is at the core of disparities in health outcomes, which the university is aware of and striving to address. As part of the UI Health system and in conjunction with Mile Square, a network of federally qualified healthcare centers across Chicago and Rockford, the Specialty Care Building is a valuable resource for those who have traditionally been underserved.

The Specialty Care Building is an essential tool in helping the U of I System fulfill its mission, to serve the state of Illinois and improve the lives of its people. The project also serves as an important economic driver for the state, with the construction project employing about 500 people and the health facility expected to generate 100 full-time jobs.

The funding for the new facility also reflects a powerful spirit of teamwork between the university and the public and private industry. By relying on P3 funding (public-private partnership), this facility and its programs have a deep and broad foundation from which to serve its communities.

PART IV
Supporting Innovation

SIEBEL CENTER FOR DESIGN
Discover the Previously Unimagined

URBANA-CHAMPAIGN

College/Department: Multi-Disciplinary
Architect: Bohlin Cywinski Jackson
Project Square Footage: 69,000 GSF
Certified LEED Gold
Project Budget: $48,000,000

When people from different countries, majors, histories, realities, and interests work side by side in open environments where collaboration is the rule, not the exception, magic can happen. The Siebel Center for Design (SCD), made possible with a $25 million gift from the Thomas and Stacey Siebel Foundation, provides a high-energy hub to enable campus and community partners to connect with one another, setting the stage for serendipity.

Human-centered design (HCD) is at the heart of the SCD, a one-of-a-kind center on the Urbana-Champaign campus. HCD identifies the unmet needs of a population and develops solutions collaboratively and iteratively. HCD is a flexible approach that allows anyone to solve problems in creative and innovative ways, using processes such as empathizing with people, brainstorming ideas, and prototyping solutions.

True to the university's status as a world-renowned research institution, SCD has created a research and assessment lab focused on the impact of HCD. SCD personnel are developing HCD-based curricula and training for K-12 educators and sharing that throughout the state.

The 69,000-square-foot project includes airy classrooms, 9,000 square feet of collaboration space, nearly 5,000 square feet dedicated to fabrication space, and even an experimental kitchen.

The main circulation route in the heart of the building features a skylit, two-story atrium. A sloping, central walkway links all the levels. This universal design feature is the centerpiece of the building making accessibility a key focus.

The LEED-Gold-certified building is open to all disciplines and majors, all departments, and more importantly, the community. Anyone can come learn about HCD, check out tools, or get help with a project.

COMPUTER DESIGN RESEARCH AND LEARNING CENTER
Progress and Potential

The UIC Computer Design Research and Learning Center (CDRLC) reflects both University of Illinois Chicago's and the state's commitment to progress and potential.

Since 2005, the UIC computer science department has grown from 187 undergraduate students to more than 1,550 students, and includes more than 20 new faculty members in the last two years alone.

UIC is Chicago's only public research university—and one of the most diverse universities in the country. The center, and the State of Illinois' funding commitment of $98 million toward construction, represents a major investment to further cement UIC's place as a national leader, propelling it into the future.

The building consolidates the currently fragmented computer science department at the College of Engineering. The layout of the building will prompt students to cross paths with one another and enhance intellectual exchange. The ability to physically connect with other students and faculty, both intentionally and serendipitously, is critical to learning and overall experience.

This new home is co-located with a large cluster of university-administered classrooms at the heart of the east campus. The building is designed to be a welcoming, inclusive, and inviting space for our diverse student body. Consistent with the University of Illinois System's strong emphasis on sustainability, the new facility is built to LEED Gold standards.

The CDRLC will be a new campus hub, serve research needs with state-of-the-art facilities, and help accommodate the rapidly increasing undergraduate enrollment in computer science.

"The computer science department is a major driver of success," says President Timothy L. Killeen. "It provides a wealth of economic and technological potential for Chicago, Illinois, and the region."

College/Department: UIC College of Engineering

Architect: Booth Hansen

Project Square Footage: 135,000 GSF

Seeking LEED Gold

Project Budget: $124,800,000

FEED TECHNOLOGY CENTER
Feeding the World, Sustainably

URBANA-CHAMPAIGN

College/Department: College of ACES
Architect: ASI Industrial
Project Square Footage: 20,250 GSF
Project Budget: $20,000,000

As the saying goes, "If you've eaten today, thank a farmer."

You could also thank the researchers and students at the University of Illinois Urbana-Champaign College of Agricultural, Consumer & Environmental Sciences (ACES). As a land-grant institution, the university has been leading the charge in advanced farming technology and research since its founding. The new Feed Technology Center will help the university continue its world-class work.

The state-of-the-art equipment and software at the Feed Technology Center replaces its 95-year-old feed mill and enables the university to advance its mission to feed the state, the country, and the world in the most sustainable manner possible. Research at the Feed Technology Center will enable the industry to produce more animal protein with less input.

Animal nutrition scientists and hundreds of undergraduate and graduate students will utilize the facility's capabilities to design and test healthy, efficient diets for livestock, poultry, and companion animals. The facility provides hands-on educational opportunities for students across the College of ACES.

In addition to serving as the site of faculty research, the Feed Technology Center offers opportunities for students to safely gain hands-on experience with the latest feed technologies, positioning them as strong contenders for leadership positions within the industry.

New undergraduate and graduate courses are being created to expand the curriculum in animal nutrition, including a new undergraduate concentration in feed processing technology.

Continuing education and workshops for feed industry employees also are offered. The programs help disseminate research findings and enable the entire industry to maintain the highest safety and production protocols, based on that research.

This close relationship between the university and its various stakeholders is reflected in the funding of the facility through a public-private partnership.

UNIVERSITY HALL
Preserving an Icon

Built in 1963, the University of Illinois Chicago's University Hall epitomizes the Brutalist style, with its concrete exterior, narrow, recessed windows, and a series of cantilevers that make the building 20 feet wider at its top than at its base. This eye-catching, 28-story building is the seat of the UIC administration and a striking addition to the skyline.

However, after 50 years, the building's concrete and reinforced steel façade had degraded. It took workers 3 years to restore and repair the concrete facade, re-roof all gallery ledges, and clean or repair ledge drains to return the building to its original appearance and prevent further water damage.

This building is not only a touchstone on the campus, it is home to a pair of nesting Peregrine falcons, a bird whose population has gradually recovered after it was decimated by DDT. University Hall is one of 14 Peregrine falcon nesting spots in Chicago. It was critical not to disturb the birds during the project, and extensive care was taken to leave them in peace.

Falcons have nested on the 28th floor since they were introduced there in 1998. The original female, Rosie, raised 32 chicks. The current female, Nitz, has used the spot—which provides high altitude, good sight lines, and cover from the weather—since 2013.

The renovation included windows that give Field Museum experts easier access to the birds, and nesting boxes made with fiberglass trays and river rock.

College/Department: University of Illinois Chicago

Architect: RATIO Architects

Project Square Footage: Exterior Work

Project Budget: $24,655,800

PART V
Athletics

With its awe-inspiring white dome glowing in the night sky, the State Farm Center (previously Assembly Hall) is a mid-century modern icon. Built in 1963, the famous concrete dome structure was designed by acclaimed architect and Urbana-Champaign alumnus Max Abramovitz.

The renovation has completely transformed the venue, while retaining the legacy and tradition of this great architectural achievement. The designers worked closely with the Illinois State Historic Preservation Office (ISHPO), to identify and celebrate the existing features of the building that make it iconic.

In addition, because of the University of Illinois System's commitment to sustainability, the renovation was built to LEED Gold standards.

The State Farm Center is, in some ways, the heartbeat of the Urbana-Champaign community. The center hosts not just Illini sporting events, but cultural events including Broadway shows and premier music acts. By making the center more user-friendly (including extra restrooms and protected space for game-day patrons to get out of the weather) and comfortable (it had no air conditioning before renovation), it continues to be a gem the entire community can benefit from.

The renovation also added a fully integrated smoke control system that allows for the use of pyrotechnics during shows.

The redesigned seating bowl pulls fans closer to the action. The Orange Krush student section has been the site of many cherished college memories. Space for those fans has been nearly doubled and encompasses three sides of the court. These updates help bolster a dynamic game-day atmosphere. The Orange Krush organization, a first of its kind in college athletics, provides students with a gathering spot for pregame activity.

STATE FARM CENTER
Transformed Yet Familiar

URBANA-CHAMPAIGN

College/Department: Division of Intercollegiate Athletics

Architect: AECOM

Project Square Footage: 500,000 GSF

Certified LEED Gold

Project Budget: $168,000,000

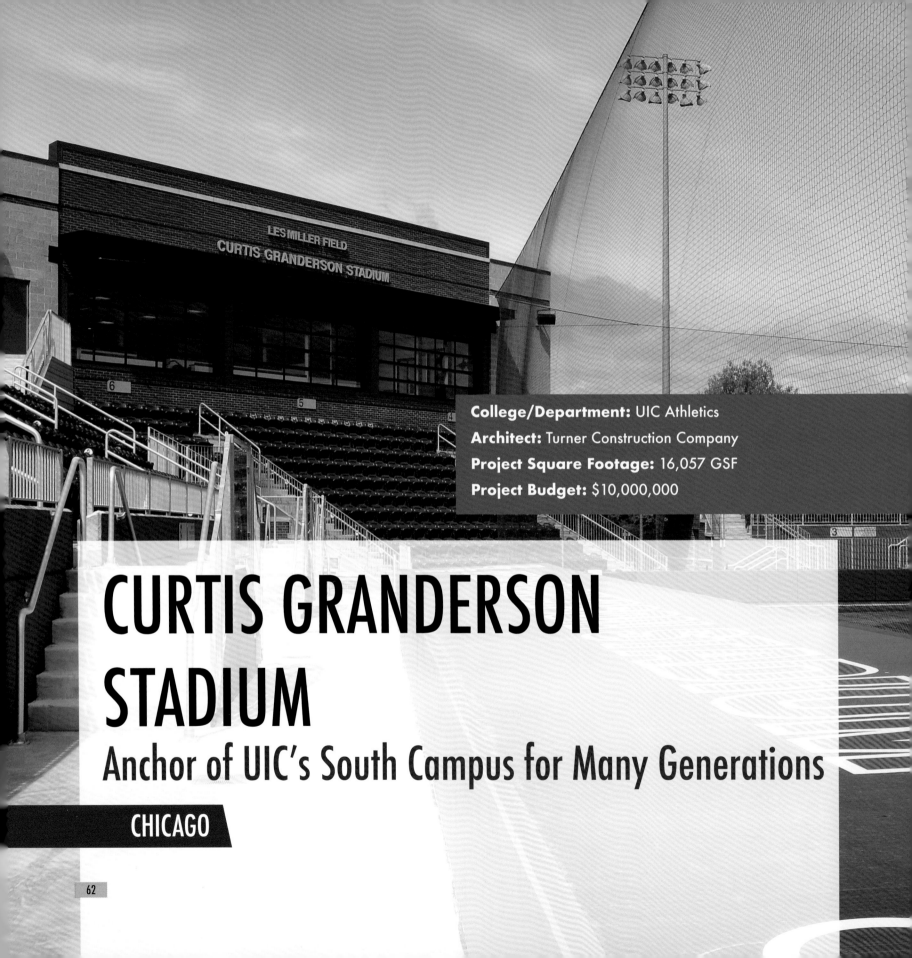

LES MILLER FIELD
CURTIS GRANDERSON STADIUM

College/Department: UIC Athletics
Architect: Turner Construction Company
Project Square Footage: 16,057 GSF
Project Budget: $10,000,000

CURTIS GRANDERSON STADIUM
Anchor of UIC's South Campus for Many Generations

CHICAGO

Opened in 2014, the Curtis Granderson Stadium at the University of Illinois Chicago is not only the new home for UIC Flames Baseball but a hub for local community sports activities.

According to *Sports Illustrated,* Granderson's gift, the largest known one-time donation from a professional athlete to their alma mater, reflects his generosity and commitment to young people. The stadium received the "Editor's Choice Award" from Ballpark Digest for its commitment to be "more than just a college ballpark."

Granderson Stadium hosts several area little league teams for games, camps, and clinics. Thousands of children throughout the Chicagoland community compete inside the state-of-the-art facility annually. This was the central motivation behind Granderson's gift: to provide a facility, not just for UIC, but for the community and, especially, local youth.

The message that using this top-quality stadium—with a capacity of 1,784, a luxury suite, press box, media suite, training room, team room, and two outdoor synthetic turf practice tunnels—sends is that Chicago youth deserve to be in the big leagues.

Granderson's nonprofit organization, Grand Kids Foundation, promotes youth development through education, physical fitness, and nutrition. He is also an enormous advocate for reading and literacy and is the author of the children's picture book, *All You Can Be: Dream It, Draw It, Become It!,* which is illustrated by fourth-grade schoolchildren.

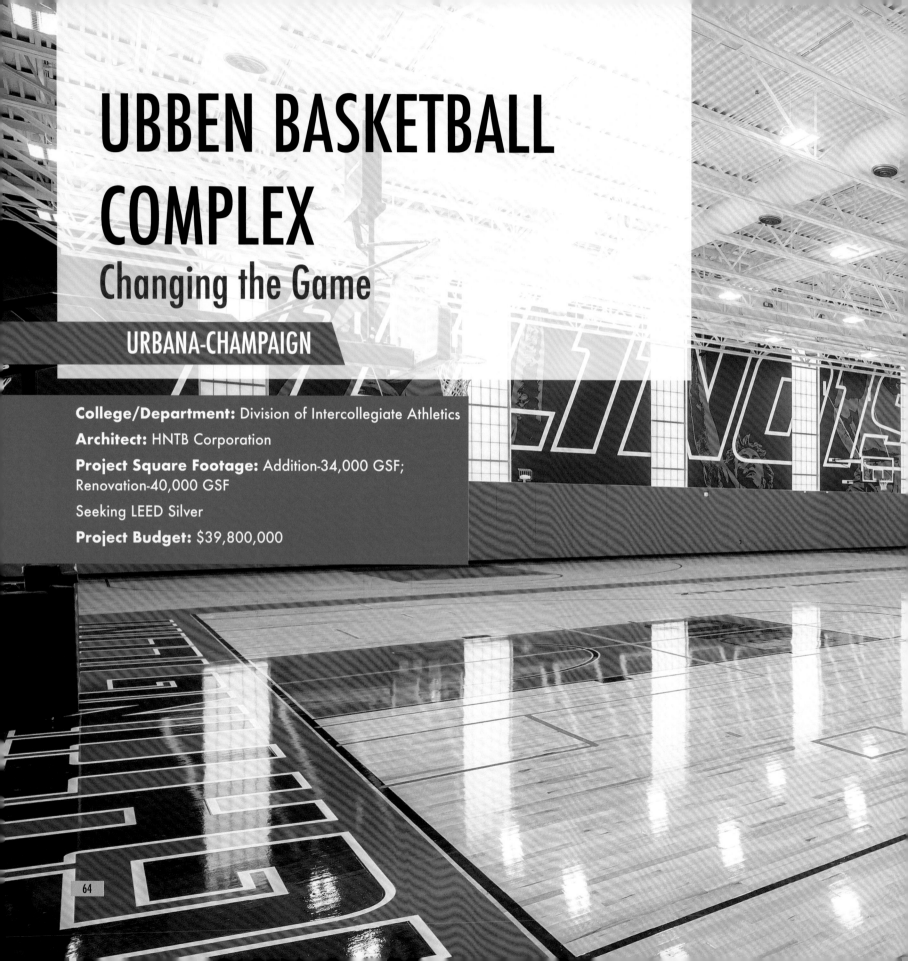

UBBEN BASKETBALL COMPLEX
Changing the Game

College/Department: Division of Intercollegiate Athletics

Architect: HNTB Corporation

Project Square Footage: Addition-34,000 GSF; Renovation-40,000 GSF

Seeking LEED Silver

Project Budget: $39,800,000

The University of Illinois Urbana-Champaign has an elite basketball program with a rich tradition.

When the Richard T. Ubben Basketball Complex opened in 1998, it was the first stand-alone basketball practice facility in college sports.

The complex demonstrated the university's commitment to excellence and to helping student-athletes reach their full potential. This facility changed the game for the basketball program, and people flew in from all over the country to admire and study it.

Now the building is undergoing a renovation that will once again make it the envy of basketball programs across the country.

While 1998 might feel like yesterday to some, it's a long time in the life of a basketball program. Today's collegiate athletic staffs are larger, technology has changed, training and preparation methods also have evolved and improved.

The renovation responds to these changing needs by adding more than 34,000 square feet to the existing facility and remodeling nearly 40,000 more square feet of existing space. Sports medicine and strength training are now far more critical in our student-athletes' regimens than in generations past. The renovated facility will include more practice space, as well as an expansive sports medicine area, including hydrotherapy and sports science spaces.

New facilities also strengthen recruiting efforts for both men's and women's basketball programs. By visiting the renovated Ubben Basketball Complex, prospective student-athletes can see at a glance the university's commitment to excellence. Successful recruiting and outstanding facilities will enable the university to continue to boast elite basketball programs.

The Henry Dale and Betty Smith Football Performance Center, located directly to the east of University of Illinois Urbana-Champaign's Memorial Stadium and connected to the existing Irwin Indoor Practice Facility, opened in August 2019.

The world-class, 107,650-square-foot, $79.2 million facility is home to the Fighting Illini football program. With expanded strength and conditioning and sports medicine space to rival any in the nation, a grand lobby showcasing Illinois football history, player development areas, expansive team locker room, and other areas for recruiting, the Football Performance Center demonstrates an institutional commitment to building, supporting, and sustaining a winning football program.

Developing a training facility as good as any in the country enables the football staff to both nurture and strengthen current players and also to successfully attract and recruit student-athletes in order to continually grow and improve Illini football.

As part of the University of Illinois System's commitment to sustainability, the facility is built to LEED Silver standards.

The new complex is the largest in the Big Ten Conference. The Center includes the Levenick Auditorium, with sweeping views of the practice fields, a nutrition center, a players' lounge complete with a game room and barber shop, and a rooftop terrace featuring an outdoor kitchen and recreational activities, including miniature golf.

The center is designed to improve individual student-athlete welfare as well as the performance of the team by providing enhanced spaces for daily use.

College/Department: Division of Intercollegiate Athletics

Architect: HNTB Corporation

Project Square Footage: 107,650 GSF

Certified LEED Silver

Project Budget: $79,200,000

HENRY DALE AND BETTY SMITH FOOTBALL PERFORMANCE CENTER

For the Win

URBANA-CHAMPAIGN

67

DEMIRJIAN PARK (SOCCER & TRACK & FIELD)

A Monumental Shift

URBANA-CHAMPAIGN

College/Department: Division of Intercollegiate Athletics

Architect: RATIO Architects

Project Square Footage: 16,800 GSF

Certified LEED Silver

Project Budget: $20,950,000

A top-quality program deserves top-quality facilities, and Demirjian Park delivers just that for both the University of Illinois Urbana-Champaign soccer and track programs. The university is now poised to host Division I and national events in both of these sports.

The stadium benefits more than 25 percent of the Fighting Illini student-athlete population by housing team facilities for women's soccer, men's track and field, and women's track and field. The investment in this new facility tells the community and the student-athletes who benefit from it that the university values their commitment to their student-athlete experiences.

In addition to the stadium, Demirjian Park (di-MER-jee-un) features two new soccer fields, one for competition and one for practice, and a renovated track and field complex. The Gary Wieneke track is named in honor of Illinois Athletics hall-of-fame track and field coach Gary Wieneke through a gift from several of Wieneke's former Fighting Illini student-athletes, some of whom competed nearly 50 years ago for him.

Demerjian Park Stadium also offers a top-of-the-line destination for regional and state-wide training and competition for youth athletes and attracts teams from throughout the Midwest. Youth athletes bring their families and fans to the Urbana-Champaign communities, providing an added economic benefit to the area.

Demirjian Park represents a monumental shift in opportunities for student-athletes, fans, and community members, whose experiences have been raised to the next level.

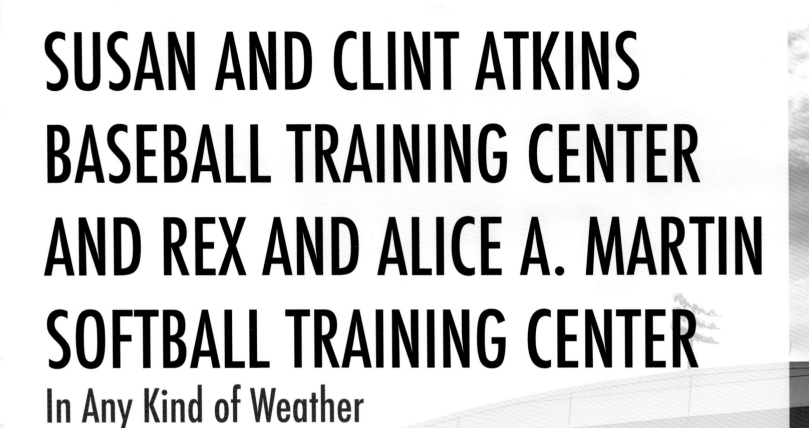

SUSAN AND CLINT ATKINS BASEBALL TRAINING CENTER AND REX AND ALICE A. MARTIN SOFTBALL TRAINING CENTER

In Any Kind of Weather

College/Department: Division of Intercollegiate Athletics

Architect: Reifsteck Reid & Company Architects

Project Square Footage: 23,500 GSF

LEED Silver—non-certified

Project Budget: $14,275,000

In order to reach their full potential, college baseball and softball players in the Midwest need an indoor training facility to enable them to hone their skills while it is cold, rainy, or even snowy outside.

The Atkins Baseball and Martin Softball training facilities are game changers, providing premier space for players to practice in game-like settings even during inclement weather. The full infield together with batting and pitching cages in both facilities enhance and strengthen the Fighting Illini programs, allowing athletes to get the jump on the competition by practicing year-round in training facilities that are the envy of the college sports community.

With its strong and dedicated fan base and skyrocketing TV viewership, by some measures, softball is the fastest growing sport in the NCAA. The Rex and Alice A. Martin Softball Training Center reflects the university's commitment to grow the sport and provide more opportunities for the outstanding athletes who compete on the diamond.

The Susan and Clint Atkins Baseball Training Center positions Illini Baseball as having one of the premier indoor baseball training facilities in college sports. The center will allow the Fighting Illini to excel at the highest level and help the program recruit many more top athletes in order to compete at the national level.

REX AND ALICE A. MARTIN SOFTBALL TRAINING CENTER

SUSAN AND CLINT ATKINS BASEBALL TRAINING CENTER

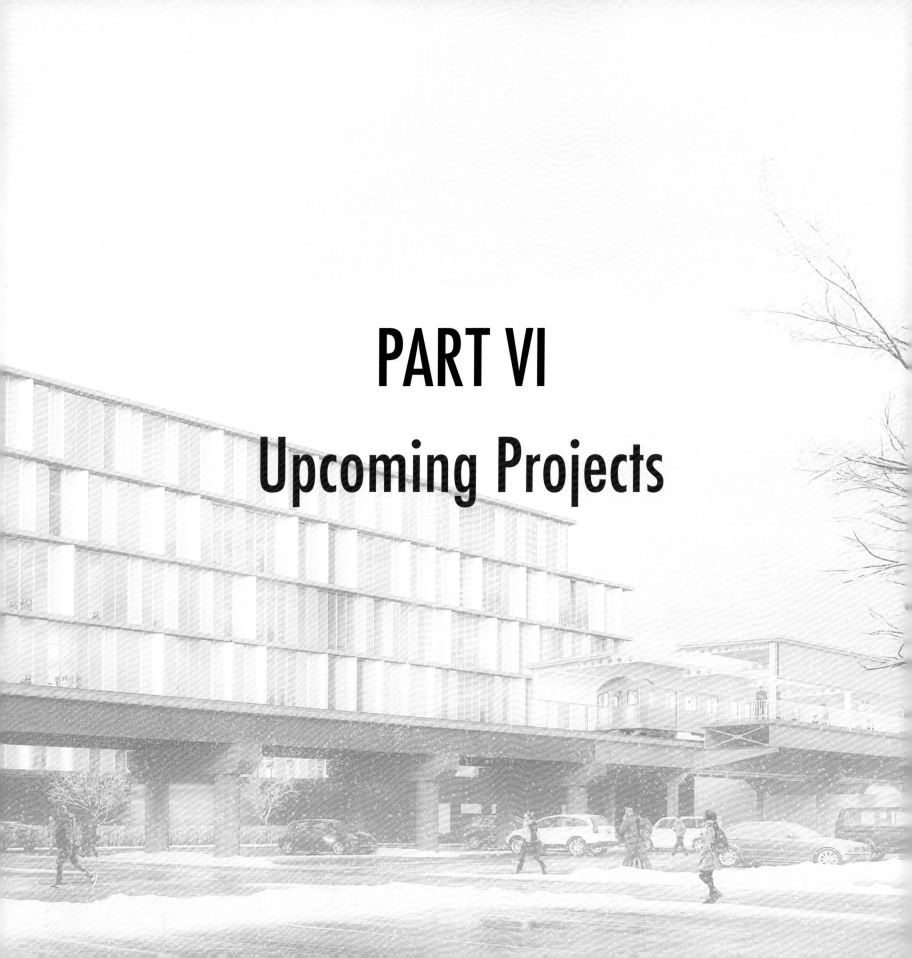

PART VI
Upcoming Projects

DISCOVERY PARTNERS INSTITUTE
Growing Talent in Illinois and Beyond

Discovery Partners Institute (DPI), a world-class education and resource center led by the University of Illinois System, is one of five Illinois Innovation Network (IIN) hubs in the Chicagoland area.

The institute's permanent space, in The 78—Chicago's most ambitious development project in a generation—signals its commitment to the city's visionary goal to create a dynamic and innovative residential, commercial, and institutional community, complete with a riverwalk, bike lanes, access to public transportation, some affordable housing, and parks and other public spaces. This groundbreaking, diverse, and exciting new neighborhood will challenge how the world thinks about Chicago and how Chicagoans think about their city.

DPI at The 78 will be a technology magnet that makes it attractive for young talent to stay—and makes it easier for companies to locate their high-tech, high-paying jobs in Chicago.

Because diversity and inclusion are primary elements of DPI's mission, intentionally designed programs to address critical challenges that have historically disadvantaged underrepresented groups in tech will be a significant focus. DPI also will partner with organizations that have relationships with underrepresented communities to build deep connections with the local tech community.

DPI will collaborate with its partners to solve complex societal challenges in the areas of food and agriculture; health and wellness; water, environment, and climate; insurance and financial services; transportation and logistics—all areas that impact not only the residents of Chicago but the entire state.

DPI at The 78 will be a magnet and catalyst for those who share the goal of retaining and encouraging the growth of the state's deep pool of homegrown tech start-ups and talent.

College/Department: Discovery Partners Institute/Illinois Innovation Network

Architect: Jacobs and OMA*AMO

Project Square Footage: 233,460 GSF

Seeking LEED Gold

Project Budget: $285,000,000

74

DRUG DISCOVERY AND CANCER RESEARCH PAVILION

Driving Innovation and Progress

The construction of the Drug Discovery and Cancer Research Pavilion (DDCRP)—a five-story facility dedicated to pharmaceutical research—represents a partnership between the University of Illinois Cancer Center, the UIC College of Pharmacy, Discovery Partners Institute, and the State of Illinois.

Located on UIC's west campus, the DDCRP is dedicated to cancer and pharmaceutical research with a focus on drug development and discovery. This new, state-of-the-art facility for emerging translational research will enhance the natural synergy between precision oncology and drug discovery.

The University of Illinois Cancer Center is among a select group of medical centers accredited by the Commission on Cancer and is also well-funded by the National Cancer Institute. The new DDCRP will provide state-of-art facilities to continue these life-saving and forward-looking efforts.

In addition to cancer therapeutics, drug discovery research will focus on critical healthcare elements such as infectious diseases and women's health.

The DDCRP's dedicated cancer research space will have a prominent street presence. Conveniently located next to the Polk Pink Line CTA station, the facility will have a strong public visibility, encouraging good relations with the local community and other clients.

With its culture of innovation and collaboration, UIC has long been a leader in pharmacology and cancer research and treatments. The UIC DDCRP will further establish the University of Illinois Chicago as a leader in providing life-saving treatments and technologies to patients—especially those in underserved populations—as well as an economic benefit to the State of Illinois.

By bringing together industry partners, education and clinical programs, research, and our community, a creative, collaborative environment to drive innovate therapeutic discovery has been created.

College/Department: College of Pharmacy/Illinois Innovation Network

Architect: Holabird and Root

Project Square Footage: 190,000 GSF

Seeking LEED Gold

Project Budget: $166,500,000

UIC INNOVATION CENTER
Learning by Doing

CHICAGO

Founded in 2011, the UIC Innovation Center provides interdisciplinary, hands-on learning and problem-solving experiences for students from multiple colleges, including Architecture, Design and the Arts, and Medicine, in collaboration with numerous industry partners.

This approach provides students with a unique learning experience in nonlinear and iterative thinking, as well as real-world insight into working at a corporation.

The Innovation Center is an educational hybrid of learning and doing, and as such it has been wildly successful. Located in the heart of the UIC campus, the Innovation Center serves as an incubator to develop and deliver ideas, products, and intellectual property in close collaboration with industry sponsors.

More than 200 students are involved in some form of interdisciplinary class, lab, or project at the Innovation Center each year. Faculty members representing 20 academic departments are currently teaching classes or directing labs and projects within the flexible use space. These projects, attracting as they do, students from all disciplines, knit the campus together.

The center has been so successful, it has outgrown its space. The new space enables the center to expand its reach both inside the UIC campus, to enable more students to take advantage of this paradigm-shifting approach to education, and to expand its appeal to corporate partners, which so far have included Caterpillar, Northern Trust, Dell Technology, the American Academy of Pediatrics, Amazon, and more than 20 others.

The Innovation Center is a storytelling space, and the expanded facility allows for presentation and exhibition spaces to tell even more stories of teamwork and success.

College/Department: Interdisciplinary

Feasibility Study: Gensler

Architect: JGMA

Project Square Footage: Addition–15,000 GSF

Anticipated LEED Silver

Project Budget: $10,000,000

CREDITS

INDEX

W

Y

Z

The University of Illinois Press
is a founding member of the
Association of University Presses.

———————————————————

Text designed by Dustin J. Hubbart
Composed in 9/12 Futura Medium
with Futura Condensed Medium display
at the University of Illinois Press

University of Illinois Press
1325 South Oak Street
Champaign, IL 61820-6903
www.press.uillinois.edu